WHY DO ANIMALS HAVE

EARS

Elizabeth Miles

Heinemann
LIBRARY

www.heinemann.co.uk/library
Visit our website to find out more information about **Heinemann Library** books.

To order:
 Phone 44 (0) 1865 888066
 Send a fax to 44 (0) 1865 314091
 Visit the Heinemann Bookshop at www.heinemann.co.uk/library to browse our catalogue and order online.

First published in Great Britain by Heinemann Library, Halley Court, Jordan Hill, Oxford
OX2 8EJ, a division of Reed Educational and Professional Publishing Ltd. Heinemann is a registered trademark of Reed Educational & Professional Publishing Limited.

OXFORD MELBOURNE AUCKLAND JOHANNESBURG BLANTYRE
GABORONE IBADAN PORTSMOUTH NH (USA) CHICAGO

Designed by David Oakley@Arnos Design
Originated by Dot Gradations
Printed in Hong Kong

ISBN 0 431 15311 6
06 05 04 03 02 01 00
10 9 8 7 6 5 4 3 2 1

British Library Cataloguing in Publication Data

Miles, Elizabeth
  Why do animals have ears
  1.Ear - Juvenile literature 2.Physiology - Juvenile
  literature
  I.Title
  573.8'9'1

Acknowledgements
The Publishers would like to thank the following for permission to reproduce photographs: BBC NHU/David Welling p. 8; BBC NHU/Ingo Arndt p. 23; BBC NHU/Anup Shah p. 21; BBC NHU/Peter Blackwell p. 13; BBC NHU/ Torsten Brehm p. 19; BBC NHU/Pete Oxford p. 28; Bruce Coleman Collection/Staffan Widstrand p. 7; Bruce Coleman Collection/Robert Maier p. 11; Bruce Coleman Collection/Dr E. Pott p. 12; Bruce Coleman Collection/Pacific Stock p. 14; Bruce Coleman Collection/Kim Taylor p. 24; Bruce Coleman Collection/Hans Reinhard pp. 6, 26; Bruce Coleman Collection/ John Cancalosi p. 29; Corbis pp. 20, 27; Corbis/Charles Philips p. 22; digital stock p. 16; digital vision p. 17, 30, and title page; OSF/Paul McCullagh p. 18; NHPA/ Anthony Bannister p. 9; NHPA/Morten Strange p. 10; OSF/Mark Hamblin p. 5; OSF/R. Okapia p. 15; OSF/K Wothe p. 25; Photodisc p. 4.

Cover photograph reproduced with permission of NHPA.

Our thanks to Claire Robinson, Head of Visitor Information and Education at London Zoo, for her help in the preparation of this book.

Every effort has been made to contact copyright holders of any material reproduced in this book. Any omissions will be rectified in subsequent printings if notice is given to the Publisher.

Contents

Words in bold, **like this**, are explained
in the Glossary.

Why do animals have ears?

People have ears, and so do many animals. We use our ears to listen to all sorts of sounds. Listen. Can you hear any sounds? Hearing helps you to be aware of the world around you.

Animal ears are different shapes and sizes.
Some rabbits have long, floppy ears. Rabbits'
ears look quite different to your ears.

Outer ears

Many animals have ears that are easy to see. The outer parts stick out. A donkey's **outer ears** collect sounds. The sounds then go into the donkey's **ear holes**.

6

Birds have no outer ears. They only have ear holes. This vulture has one hole on each side of its head. Sounds go into the holes so the bird can hear them.

Pointed ears

The lynx has pointed ears, shaped like **triangles**. Tufts of hair grow from the tips. The tufts help the lynx to hear when it is hunting in the long grass.

Aardvarks' ears are long and pointed to help them hear. These animals are **nocturnal**. They spend the night hunting for **insects** to eat. They can hear the sounds of insects called **termites** in a nest.

Rounded ears

The slow loris has rounded ears, shaped like little shells. Its ears gather sounds from the forest. The slow loris uses its **sense** of hearing and of smell to search for birds and **insects** to eat.

Mice use their rounded ears to hear each other's squeaks. Baby mice squeak to their mother. The mother mouse listens to make sure they are safe.

Big ears

Elephants in Africa have the biggest ears of any **mammal**. They use them to listen to the calls of other elephants. They flap their ears to keep cool, too.

At night, foxes use their ears to hunt for food in the dark. A bat-eared fox has big, **sensitive** ears. Its sharp hearing helps it to find **insects** to eat.

Small ears

Sea lions live and hunt in the sea. They have tiny ears. These do not stick out and slow them down when they swim. You can just see their small **outer ears**.

A hippopotamus has tiny ears that it can close. To keep cool, hippos spend lots of time in rivers and lakes. They close their ears to stop the water getting in.

Hidden ears

Birds' ears are often hidden under their feathers. They only have an **ear hole** on each side of their head. Birds listen to each other's songs and calls.

Some animals' ears are completely hidden.
A snake does not have ear holes. As a
snake cannot hear very well, it relies on
other **senses** such as sight and smell.

Ears on top

Many animals have ears on the top of their head. When zebras are busy drinking or **grazing**, their ears help them listen for danger. If they hear a **predator** coming, they quickly run away.

A hare has tall ears on the top of its head. It sits very still with its tall ears sticking up above the grass. It listens out for predators, such as a fox.

Ears at the sides

Monkeys and apes have ears at the sides of their head. Howler monkeys often listen to each other calling. They shout to other **troops** so that they keep away.

African buffalo have ears that stick out at the sides. Huge curved horns stand out above their ears. If a buffalo hears a lion, it may chase it away with its sharp horns.

Moving ears

Many animals raise their **outer ears** when they are listening carefully. It helps them hear better. Sheep dogs do this when they listen to orders from the **shepherd**.

Many animals, such as kangaroos, can turn each ear in a different direction. By doing this, they can work out where a sound is coming from.

Ears in the dark

Many **nocturnal** animals use their ears to help find their **prey** in the dark. The long-eared bat's ears help it to find moths to eat. It also listens for **echoes** to find its way.

Kiwis are nocturnal birds that cannot fly.
They cannot see each other in the long
undergrowth, so they use their ears to listen
out for each other's calls.

Underwater ears

You cannot see fishes' ears. They are hidden inside their heads. They can hear well through the water. Catfish have very good hearing. They can even hear noises made on the shore.

Trout hear very well. Some trout swim off when they hear someone getting into the water. If they hear a **predator**, they swim away to safety.

Ears on legs!

Insects have their ears in unusual places. Crickets have ears on their front legs. They use them to hear and find other crickets in the undergrowth.

Instead of ears, a spider uses hairs to pick up sounds. Rows of special hairs on its legs pick up **vibrations**. These tell the spider if a moving animal is large or small. If it is large, the spider might hide.

Fact file

- Dogs' ears can hear sounds that people cannot hear. They can hear very high sounds, like the sounds of a whistle.

- A bird can hear the sound of its own chick, even amongst a large flock of other singing birds and chicks.

- Crocodiles have ears on top of their head. They can lie in the water with their ears sticking out. This means they can hear while hiding.

Eastern grey kangaroos have a good sense of hearing.

Glossary

ear hole   part of an ear that sound travels into

echoes   sounds, such as a shout, that come back through the air

grazing   eating low-growing grass and plants

insect   small animal with three main parts to its body and six legs

mammal   animal that feeds its babies with the mothers milk. People are mammals.

nocturnal   awake and active at night, not during the day

outer ear   the part of an ear that sticks out from the head

predator   animal that hunts other animals for food

prey   animals hunted as food

sense   way of being aware of the world (seeing, hearing, smelling, touching and tasting are senses)

sensitive   pick up sounds easily

shepherd   person who looks after sheep

triangle   shape with three corners

troop   group of monkeys

vibrations   tiny movements, made by sounds

Index

Titles in the *Why Do Animals Have* series include:

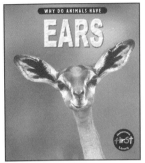

Hardback 0431 15311 6

Hardback 0431 15310 8

Hardback 0431 15326 4

Hardback 0431 15323 X

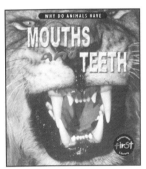

Hardback 0431 15314 0

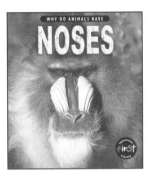

Hardback 0431 15312 4

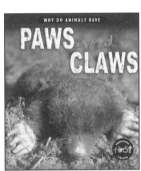

Hardback 0431 15322 1

Hardback 0431 15325 6

Hardback 0431 15313 2

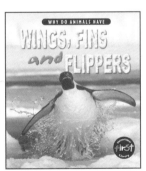

Hardback 0431 15324 8

Find out about the other titles in this series on our website www.heinemann.co.uk/library